I0802839

My First Animal Books

BORN IN THE WILD

Kelli Hicks

TABLE OF CONTENTS

A Crabtree Seedlings Book

Crabtree Publishing

crabtreebooks.com

Born in the Wild

A baby fox **howls** for its mother.

A baby fox is called a pup, or a kit.

Baby owls are covered in **down**.

Baby owls are called owlets.

Baby **opossums** hitch a ride.

A baby opossum is called a joey.

A baby deer hides in the **leaves**.

A baby deer is called a fawn.

Baby bears are called cubs.

Baby bears like to play.
Do you?

Glossary

down (DOUN): Down is a layer of very soft, fine feathers.

howls (HOULZ): When an animal howls, it makes a long, loud cry.

leaves (LEEVZ): Leaves grow on trees. In autumn, leaves turn brown and fall to the ground.

opossums (uh-POSS-uhmz): Opossums are furry animals. Opossum moms carry their babies in a pouch until they are old enough to hitch a ride.

Index

School-to-Home Support for Caregivers and Teachers

This book helps children grow by letting them practice reading. Here are a few guiding questions to help the reader build his or her comprehension skills. Possible answers appear here in red.

Before Reading

- **What do I think this book is about?** I think this book is about baby animals that are born in the wild. I think this book is about baby animals and their mothers.
- **What do I want to learn about this topic?** I want to learn more about where animals are born. I want to learn if animals are born in very cold weather.

During Reading

- **I wonder why...** I wonder why baby bears are called cubs. I wonder why baby owls are covered with very soft fine feathers.
- **What have I learned so far?** I have learned that a baby deer is called a fawn. I have learned that a baby fox is called a pup, or a kit.

After Reading

- **What details did I learn about this topic?** I have learned that different words are used to describe baby animals than those used to describe adult animals. I have learned that baby opossums like to ride on their mother's back.
- **Read the book again and look for the glossary words.** I see the word *down* on page 6, and the word *leaves* on page 14. The other glossary words are found on pages 22 and 23.

Crabtree Publishing

crabtreebooks.com 800-387-7650

Copyright © 2022 Crabtree Publishing

All rights reserved. No part of this publication may be reproduced, stored in a retrieval system or be transmitted in any form or by any means, electronic, mechanical, photocopying, recording, or otherwise, without the prior written permission of Crabtree Publishing Company. In Canada: We acknowledge the financial support of the Government of Canada through the Canada Book Fund for our publishing activities.

Published in Canada
Crabtree Publishing
616 Welland Avenue
St. Catharines, Ontario
L2M 5V6

Published in the United States
Crabtree Publishing
347 Fifth Avenue
Suite 1402-145
New York, NY 10016

Written by: Kelli Hicks
Print book version produced jointly with Blue Door Education in 2023

Photo Credits: Cover and page 13 © Jay Ondreicka, pages 3 and 5 © critterbiz, pages 7 and 9 © Kurit afshen, page 11 © Evelyn D. Harrison, page 15 © JanaHnizdilova, page 17 © Edistolady, page 19 © Volodymyr Burdiak, page 21 © Ghost Bear; All photos from Shutterstock.com

Library and Archives Canada
Cataloguing in Publication
Available at the Library and Archives Canada

Library of Congress
Cataloging-in-Publication Data
Available at the Library of Congress

Hardcover 978-1-0396-6024-3
Paperback 978-1-0396-6219-3

Printed in Canada/022024/
CP20240215